Mar 2018

Holiday Baking PARTY!

Let's Bake Fourth of July Treats!

By Ruth Owen

Gareth Stevens
PUBLISHING

Published in 2018 by Gareth Stevens Publishing
111 East 14th Street, Suite 349, New York, NY 10003

First Edition

Produced for Gareth Stevens Publishing by Ruby Tuesday Books Ltd
Designers: Tammy West and Emma Randall

Photo Credits:
Courtesy of Ruby Tuesday Books and Shutterstock.
Page 4 (right) courtesy of Alamy.

Cataloging-in-Publication Data

Names: Owen, Ruth.
Title: Let's bake Fourth of July treats! / Ruth Owen.
Description: New York : Gareth Stevens Publishing, 2018. | Series: Holiday baking party | Includes index.
Identifiers: LCCN ISBN 9781538213285 (pbk.) | ISBN 9781538213308 (library bound) | ISBN 9781538213292 (6 pack)
Subjects: LCSH: Fourth of July--Juvenile literature. | Fourth of July celebrations--Juvenile literature. |
Holiday cooking--Juvenile literature. | Desserts--Juvenile literature.
Classification: LCC TX739.2.F68 O94 2018 | DDC 641.5'68--dc23

Manufactured in the United States of America

CPSIA compliance information: Batch #CW18GS: For further information contact Gareth Stevens, New York, New York at 1-800-542-2595.

Contents

Let's Get Baking!

It's almost July 4th, so this year celebrate Independence Day by treating your family to home-baked cookies, cakes, and pies. The recipes in this book use delicious summery ingredients such as strawberries and blueberries. They also incorporate fun **symbols** of the big day such as stars, stripes, and even hot dogs!

So get ready for this year's picnic, cookout, or party by inviting some friends to drop by your kitchen. Then get busy mixing, frosting, and decorating—let's have a holiday baking party!

Get Ready to Bake

- Before cooking, always wash your hands well with soap and hot water.
- Make sure the kitchen countertop and all your equipment is clean.
- Read the recipe carefully before you start cooking. If you don't understand a step, ask an adult to help you.
- Gather together all the ingredients and equipment you will need. Baking is more fun when you're prepared!

Measuring cup

Measuring spoons

Measuring Counts

- Make sure you measure your ingredients carefully. If you get a measurement wrong, it could affect how successful your baking is.
  - Use measuring scales or a measuring cup to measure dry and liquid ingredients.
  - Measuring spoons can be used to measure small amounts of ingredients.

Have Fun, Stay Safe!

It's very important to have an adult around whenever you do any of the following tasks in the kitchen:

- Using a mixer, the stovetop burners, or an oven.
- Using sharp utensils, such as knives and vegetable peelers or corers.
- Working with heated pans, pots, or baking sheets. Always use oven mitts when handling heated pans, pots, or baking sheets.

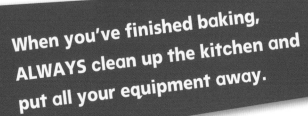

When you've finished baking, ALWAYS clean up the kitchen and put all your equipment away.

The quantities on this page will make 20 cookies.

Star-Spangled Cookies

Get your holiday baking party off to a great start by making some sugary, buttery cookies that are decorated with red, white, and blue sprinkles.

Ingredients:

To make the cookie dough:

- 1 ½ cups all-purpose flour (plus a little extra for dusting)
- ½ cup superfine sugar
- 5 ounces butter (plus a little for greasing)

For the frosting and decorations:

- 1 cup powdered sugar
- 1 cup water
- Your choice of red, white, and blue sprinkles

Equipment:

- 2 large cookie sheets
- Mixing bowl
- Wooden spoon
- Plastic wrap
- Rolling pin
- 3-inch (7.5-cm) star-shaped cookie cutter
- Oven mitts
- 2 potholders
- Wire rack for cooling
- Sieve
- Small bowl
- Spoon (for mixing frosting)
- Brush

Step 1 Grease the cookie sheets with a little butter to keep your cookies from sticking to the sheets.

Step 2 Put the butter and sugar into the mixing bowl and **cream together** with the wooden spoon until smooth and fluffy.

Step 3 Add the flour and mix the ingredients with the spoon. Next, use your hands to rub and combine the ingredients until the mixture looks like breadcrumbs.

Finally, use your hands to squeeze and **knead** the mixture to make a ball of soft dough.

Dough

Step 4 Wrap the dough in plastic wrap and place in a refrigerator for 30 minutes.

Step 5 **Preheat** the oven to 350°F (180°C).

Step 6 Dust your countertop with a little flour. Unwrap the dough and place on the dusted surface. Use a rolling pin to roll out the dough to about ¼ inch (6 mm) thick.

Step 7 Cut as many star shapes as you can from the dough and place them on the cookie sheets.

Step 8 Bake the cookies for about 15 minutes, or until they are turning golden. The centers of the cookies will still be slightly soft, but they'll soon firm up.

Remove the cookie sheets from the oven with oven mitts and stand the sheets on the potholders. Allow the cookies to cool for about 10 minutes, and then carefully place each cookie on a wire rack and allow to cool completely.

Step 9

Use the sieve to sift the powdered sugar into the small bowl. Little by little, add water and mix to make a simple, white frosting. The frosting should be thick, but you must be able to brush it onto the cookies.

Step 10

Brush each cookie with a little frosting. Then scatter some sprinkles over the frosting while it is still wet. Gently shake off any excess sprinkles and allow the frosting to set.

Enjoy sharing your star-spangled cookies with your family and friends.

Marbled Cupcakes

The quantities on this page will make 12 cupcakes.

These delightful Fourth of July cupcakes have red and blue marbled cake topped off with frosting, sprinkles, and other decorations. Bake your cupcakes and then get creative frosting and decorating with your friends.

Ingredients:

To make the cupcake batter:
- 7 ounces butter or margarine
- 1 cup superfine sugar
- 2 cups cake flour
- 1 teaspoon baking powder
- ¼ teaspoon salt
- 3 large eggs
- ½ cup milk
- ½ teaspoon vanilla extract
- Red and blue gel food coloring

For the decorations and frosting:
- 2 ½ cups powdered sugar
- 1 cup butter
- 4 tablespoons milk
- White gel food coloring
- Your choice of red, white, and blue decorations

Equipment:
- 1 12-hole or 2 6-hole muffin pans
- 12 muffin cases
- Mixing bowl
- Wooden spoon
- Electric mixer (optional)
- 2 small bowls
- Spoons for mixing
- Metal skewer
- Oven mitts
- Potholder
- 3 small bowls (for frosting)
- Frosting gun

Step 1 Preheat the oven to 350°F (180°C).

Step 2 Line the muffin pan with the muffin cases.

Step 3 Put the butter and sugar into the mixing bowl and cream together with a wooden spoon until fluffy. If you wish, you can use an electric mixer for this step.

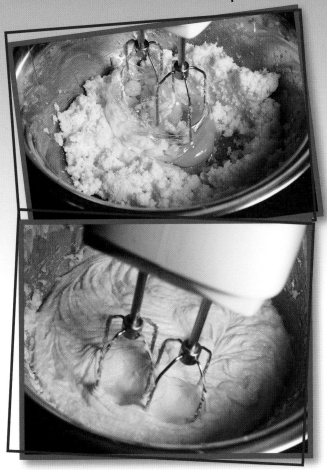

Step 4 Add the eggs, flour, baking powder, salt, milk, and vanilla extract to the bowl. Use a wooden spoon or electric mixer to **beat** the ingredients together until the mixture is thick and smooth.

Step 5 Share the cupcake batter equally between the mixing bowl and two additional bowls. The amounts don't have to be exact.

Step 6 Leave one bowl of batter as a natural yellow color. Add red coloring to the second bowl and blue to the third bowl. Add the gel coloring in a tiny blob (about half the size of your pinkie fingernail). Keep adding and mixing until you have a strong, bright color.

step 7
Spoon the three colors of batter into the muffin cases.

step 8
To create the marbling effect inside your cupcakes, take a metal skewer and make a cross through the batter in each muffin case. This will slightly swirl the three colors of batter into each other.

step 9
Bake the cakes for 20 minutes, or until they have risen above the edges of the muffin cases. To test if the cakes are baked, insert a metal skewer into one cake. If it comes out clean, the cakes are ready.

Use oven mitts to remove the pan from the oven and stand it on a potholder. Allow the cakes to cool completely.

Marbled effect

Step 10
To make the frosting, mix the powdered sugar, butter, and milk together until thick and smooth.

Step 11
Divide the frosting between three small bowls. Carefully add white coloring to one bowl, red to the second, and blue to the third.

Step 12
Working with one color at a time, spoon the frosting into a frosting gun. Gently create a swirled effect on the top of four cupcakes. Repeat with the red and white frosting.

Step 13
Add sprinkles and other decorations.

Ingredients:

- 1 ½ cups all-purpose flour
- ½ cup superfine sugar
- 5 ounces butter (plus a little for greasing)
- 1 teaspoon vanilla extract
- Orange gel food coloring
- Tube of yellow frosting

Equipment:

- Large cookie sheet
- Mixing bowl
- Wooden spoon
- Small bowl
- Plastic wrap
- Oven mitts
- Potholder
- Wire rack for cooling
- Small serrated knife

Hot Dog Cookies

Enjoying a scrumptious hot dog is an important part of any Fourth of July celebration. This year, WOW your friends and family by baking these fun look-alike cookies that turn hot dogs into a crunchy, sweet treat!

Step 1
Grease the cookie sheet with a little butter to keep your cookies from sticking to the sheet.

Step 2
Put the butter and sugar into the mixing bowl and cream together with a wooden spoon until smooth and fluffy.

Superfine sugar

Cake flour

Vanilla extract

Butter

Step 3
Add the flour and vanilla extract and mix the ingredients with the spoon. Next, use your hands to rub and combine the ingredients until the mixture looks like breadcrumbs.

Step 4
Separate off a third of the mixture and put it into a small bowl.

Orange dough

Add a pea-sized blob of orange food coloring to the crumbly mixture. Gently rub and work the mixture with your fingers so the color spreads evenly. Add more color as needed to obtain a strong hot dog orange.

Finally, squeeze the mixture into a ball of dough.

step 5 Wash any coloring from your hands and then squeeze the rest of the crumbly mixture into a second larger ball.

step 6 Wrap both balls of dough in plastic wrap and place in a refrigerator for 30 minutes.

step 7 Preheat the oven to 350°F (180°C).

step 8 Unwrap the balls of dough. Cut the large, uncolored ball of dough into eight equal chunks.

step 9 To make the hot dog buns, take a chunk of dough, gently roll it into a ball, and then roll the ball into a short sausage shape. Flatten and squeeze the sausage shape to make an oval of dough that's about half an inch (1.25 cm) thick.

Hot dog bun

Chunk of dough

Sausage shape

Ball

Use your finger to make a dent in the bun shape.

step 10 Cut the orange dough into eight pieces. Roll each piece into a hot dog sausage and gently press it onto a bun.

step 11
Place the hot dog cookies on the greased cookie sheet.

step 12
Bake the cookies for about 15 minutes, or until they are turning golden at the edges. The centers of the cookies will still be slightly soft, but they'll soon firm up.

step 13
Remove the cookies from the oven with an oven mitt and place the cookie sheet on a potholder. Allow to cool for about 10 minutes, and then carefully place each cookie on a wire rack and allow to cool completely.

Browned, rough edge

step 14
When the cookies are cooled, you can carefully trim off any browned or rough edges with a serrated knife.

Yellow frosting

Add a generous trickle of yellow frosting to look like mustard.

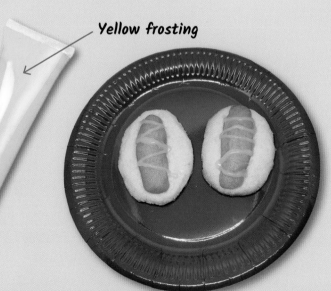

Your hot dog cookies are ready to present to your guests at your Fourth of July cookout!

The quantities on this page will make 12 cupcakes.

Ingredients:

To make the cupcake batter:
- 4 tablespoons boiling water
- ½ cup cocoa powder
- 3 eggs
- 6 ounces butter or margarine
- 1 cup golden superfine sugar
- 1 cup cake flour
- 1 teaspoon baking powder

For the decorations and frosting:
- 1 cup strawberries
- ½ cup raspberries
- ½ cup blueberries
- 2 ½ cups powdered sugar
- 1 ½ ounces butter
- 4 ounces cream cheese
- White gel coloring for frosting

Equipment:
- 1 12-hole or 2 6-hole muffin pans
- 12 muffin cases
- Sieve
- Mixing bowl
- Wooden spoon
- Hand whisk
- Electric mixer (optional)
- Metal skewer
- Oven mitts
- Potholder
- Small knife
- Paper towel
- Small bowl
- Spoon for mixing

Summer Berry Chocolate Cupcakes

Red and blue berries, smooth, white cream cheese frosting, and a delicious chocolate cupcake are combined in this next recipe. The colors will look fantastic at your Fourth of July picnic, and the combination of lush chocolate and fruit is just delicious!

18

step 1 Preheat the oven to 400°F (200°C).

step 2 Line the muffin pan with muffin cases.

step 3 Use the sieve to sift the cocoa powder into the mixing bowl. Pour in the boiling water and mix into a thick **paste**.

Cocoa powder

Hand whisk

step 4 Add the eggs, butter, sugar, flour, and baking powder. Use the wooden spoon, a hand whisk, or an electric mixer to beat the ingredients together until the mixture is thick and smooth.

step 5 Divide the mixture equally between the 12 muffin cases.

Step 6

Bake the cakes for 12 to 15 minutes, or until they have risen above the edges of the muffin cases. To test if the cakes are baked, insert a metal skewer into one cake. If it comes out clean, the cakes are ready.

Use oven mitts to remove the pan from the oven and stand it on a potholder. Allow the cakes to cool completely.

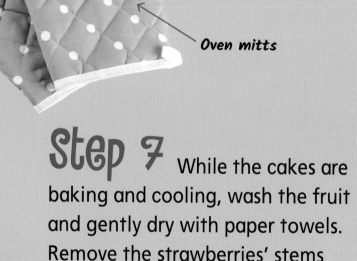

Baked cupcakes

Oven mitts

Step 7

While the cakes are baking and cooling, wash the fruit and gently dry with paper towels. Remove the strawberries' stems and cut into slices.

Step 8

To make the frosting, mix the powdered sugar, butter, and cream cheese together until thick and smooth.

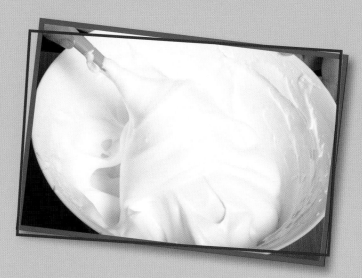

Step 9

The cream cheese frosting will be a creamy, slightly off-white color. To get a bright white frosting you can use white coloring. Add about a quarter of a teaspoon of coloring at a time and mix thoroughly until the frosting turns white.

Step 10

Spoon some frosting onto the top of each cake and swirl with a spoon.

Step 11

Finally, decorate each cupcake with some fruit.

Enjoy!

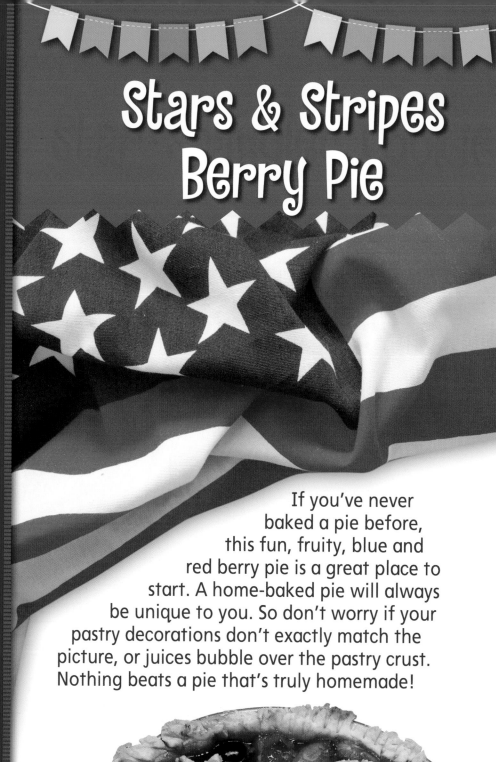

Ingredients:

For the pastry:
- 2 cups all-purpose flour (plus a little extra for dusting)
- ¼ cup ground almonds
- ¼ teaspoon salt
- 5 ounces butter or margarine
- Up to 7 tablespoons cold water
- 1 egg
- 1 tablespoon brown sugar

For the pie filling:
- 3 ½ cups chopped strawberries (washed)
- 1 ½ cups raspberries (washed)
- 2 cups blueberries (washed)
- ½ cup superfine sugar
- ¼ cup corn starch
- 1 tablespoon water

Equipment:
- Mixing bowl
- Plastic wrap
- Small sharp knife
- Rolling pin
- 1 9-inch (23-cm) pie dish
- Aluminum foil
- 1-inch (2.5-cm) star-shaped cookie cutter
- 4 medium bowls
- Spoon
- Fork
- Brush
- Oven mitts
- Potholder

Stars & Stripes Berry Pie

If you've never baked a pie before, this fun, fruity, blue and red berry pie is a great place to start. A home-baked pie will always be unique to you. So don't worry if your pastry decorations don't exactly match the picture, or juices bubble over the pastry crust. Nothing beats a pie that's truly homemade!

step 1 Preheat the oven to 425°F (220°C).

step 2 Put the flour, ground almonds, and salt into the mixing bowl. Add the butter, cut into small chunks. Using your fingers, **rub in** the butter to the dry ingredients until the mixture looks like breadcrumbs.

Breadcrumb-like mixture

step 3 Adding the water a little at a time, gently squeeze and knead the breadcrumb-like mixture until it becomes a ball of pastry dough. Once you have made a soft dough, stop adding water.

step 4 Wrap the ball of dough in plastic wrap and put in the refrigerator for about 20 minutes.

step 5 In a small bowl, mix together the sugar and cornstarch.

step 6 Put the blueberries, a tablespoon of water, and ¼ cup of sugar and cornstarch mixture into a bowl. Mix until the blueberries are coated.

step 7 Put the remaining sugar and cornstarch, strawberries, and raspberries into another bowl and mix until the fruit is coated with the mixture.

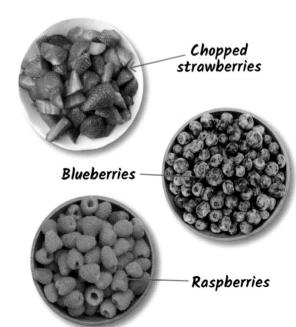

Chopped strawberries

Blueberries

Raspberries

23

step 8

Unwrap the ball of dough, cut off one-third, and place to one side. Dust your work surface with a little flour. Use a rolling pin to roll out the large piece of dough until it is big enough to fill your pie dish.

Lay the dough in the pie dish and press firmly into the bottom and sides.

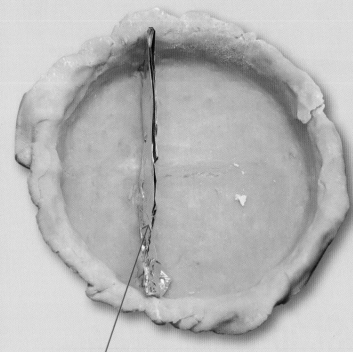

Aluminum foil barrier

step 9

Fold some aluminum foil and create a barrier one-third of the way across the pie dish.

step 10

Pour the red fruits into the large section of pie and the blueberries into the smaller section. Gently press the fruit into place with a spoon, and then remove the foil barrier.

Step 11
Roll out the remaining piece of dough. Use a small knife and a star-shaped cutter to make your stars and stripes, and then lay them on top of the fruit. Trim and tidy up the pie's crust and press a fork into the crust to crimp it.

Step 12
In a small bowl, use the fork to whisk up an egg and then brush the egg over the pastry. This will turn the pastry a golden brown when it's baked. Finally, sprinkle a little crunchy brown sugar over the pie.

Step 13
Bake the pie for 35 to 45 minutes. The fruit will be bubbling hot and the pastry should have turned a golden brown color.

Step 14
Use oven mitts to take the pie from the oven and stand it on a potholder to cool before serving.

The quantities on this page will make one large frosted cake with four layers.

Ingredients:

To make the cupcake batter:
- 2 cups cake flour
- 2 teaspoons baking powder
- 8 ounces soft, unsalted butter or margarine (plus extra for greasing)
- 1 cup superfine sugar
- 4 large eggs
- 1 tablespoon vanilla extract
- ¼ cup milk
- Red and blue food coloring gel

To make the frosting:
- 3 ½ ounces butter
- 8 ½ ounces cream cheese
- 5 cups powdered sugar (sieved)
- White gel coloring for frosting
- Red, white, and blue sprinkles and decorations

Equipment:
- 2 7-inch (18-cm) cake pans
- 2 mixing bowls
- Wooden spoon
- Electric mixer (optional)
- Spoons for mixing
- Rubber spatula
- Oven mitts
- Metal skewer
- Wire racks for cooling
- Sieve
- Medium bowl
- Spoon for mixing frosting
- Serrated knife
- A plate for serving

26

Fourth of July Layer Cake

This amazing layer cake will make a stunning centerpiece for your holiday picnic or party table. It looks complicated, but it's easy to bake, frost, and assemble. Once your red, white, and blue layers are in place, unleash your creativity with holiday-themed sprinkles, candies, and decorations.

Step 1
Grease the two cake pans with a little butter to keep your cakes from sticking. You will be baking the four layers two at a time.

Step 2
Preheat the oven to 350°F (180°C).

Greased pan

Step 3
Put the butter and sugar into a mixing bowl and cream together with a wooden spoon until fluffy. If you wish, you can use an electric mixer for steps 3, 4, and 5.

Step 4
Add the eggs to the bowl one at a time and gently beat into the mixture.

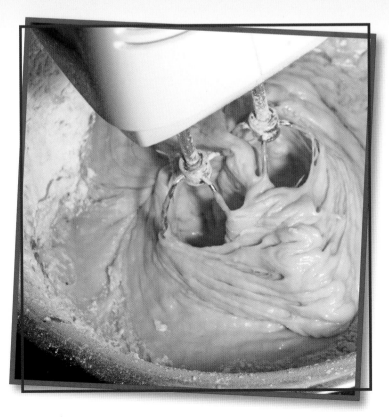

Step 5
Add the flour, baking powder, and vanilla extract and beat until thoroughly combined. The mixture should be a thick liquid. If it's stiff and won't pour, add milk a little at a time until the mixture becomes a thick liquid.

Step 6
Put half the cake batter into the second mixing bowl.

Step 7
Now add red food coloring to one bowl and blue to the other. Add the gel in a tiny blob (about half the size of your pinkie fingernail) and gently mix. Keep adding color until you have the shade you want.

Step 8
Use a spatula to scoop the red batter into the two cake pans, dividing it equally. Smooth the top of the batter with the spatula.

Step 9
Bake the two red layers in the center of the oven for 20 minutes. To test if the cakes are baked, insert a metal skewer into one cake. If it comes out clean, the cakes are ready. Use oven mitts to remove the pans from the oven and stand them on wire racks.

After about 10 minutes, carefully remove the cakes from the pans and place them back on the racks to cool.

Step 10
Wash and re-grease the pans and then repeat steps 8 and 9 with the blue batter.

Step 11
To make the frosting, use a spoon or electric mixer to combine the sieved powdered sugar, butter, and cream cheese together until thick and smooth. Add the white frosting color little by little, mixing well until the frosting turns white.

Step 12
To reveal the bright colors inside the cake layers, trim the outer edge, or crust, from the side of each cake. Use a serrated knife to do this, carefully slicing off just a paper-thin layer of cake.

Step 13
To assemble the cake, place a red layer on the serving plate. If the cake has risen unevenly or is slightly domed, use a serrated knife to slice off any high points and create a flat surface. Smear on a thick layer of frosting with a spatula.

Serrated knife

Happy Fourth of July!

Step 14
Place the blue layer on top of the frosting. Keep adding the layers with frosting sandwiched between them.

Step 15
Once the fourth layer (blue) is in place, smear a layer of frosting on top of the cake and top off with sprinkles and your choice of decorations.

Glossary

beat

To blend a mixture of ingredients until they are smooth with equipment such as a spoon, fork, hand whisk, or electric mixer.

cream together

To beat butter or margarine, usually with sugar, to make it light and fluffy.

knead

To press, squeeze, and fold dough with your hands to make it smooth and stretchy.

paste

A thick, soft, moist substance that can be stirred or spread. A paste is usually made by mixing dry ingredients with a small amount of liquid.

preheat

To turn on an oven so it is at the correct temperature for cooking a particular dish before the food is placed inside.

rub in

To use the fingers to rub flour (or other dry ingredients) into a fat, such as butter. This technique creates a breadcrumb-like mixture that is used to make pastry, crumbles, or scones.

symbols

Objects or pictures that stand for or represent another thing, such as an important event or person. For example, stars are a symbol of the Fourth of July.

Index

Further Information

Steele, Victoria. *101 Quick & Easy Cupcake and Muffin Recipes*.
CreateSpace Independent Publishing Platform, 2014.

Learn more about the Fourth of July here!
https://www.dkfindout.com/us/more-find-out/festivals-and-holidays/
independence-day/